HOW TO WRITE THE PERFECT COVER LETTER: A STEP-BY-STEP GUIDE

Aline An

CONTENTS

INTRODUCTION

Welcome to "How to Write the Perfect Cover Letter: A Step-by-Step Guide," your essential roadmap to crafting a cover letter that not only complements your resume but significantly boosts your job application. In the competitive job market, standing out to potential employers is more crucial than ever. While your resume provides a snapshot of your professional background, a well-written cover letter offers you the chance to speak directly to your future employer, showcasing your personality and enthusiasm for the role.

A cover letter is not just a formality; it's an opportunity. It allows you to explain in your own words why you're the perfect fit for the job, highlight your most relevant skills and experiences, and demonstrate your knowledge of the company and its values. This guide is designed to walk you through the process of creating a compelling cover letter that resonates with hiring managers and makes them eager to meet you. Whether you're a seasoned professional or entering the job market for the first time, mastering the art of the cover letter is a powerful tool in your job search arsenal. Let's dive in and discover how you can make your application shine.

UNDERSTANDING THE PURPOSE OF A COVER LETTER

The Role of a Cover Letter in Your Job Hunt

A cover letter is your personal introduction to a potential employer, serving as a companion to your resume. While your resume outlines your professional qualifications and experiences, your cover letter gives you the opportunity to explain in your own words why you're the perfect candidate for the job. Think of it as a chance to tell a story that your resume can't—a way to show not just what you've done, but who you are.

In the job application process, the cover letter plays a crucial role. It's your first point of contact with an employer, offering a glimpse into your personality, enthusiasm, and professional demeanor. More than just a formality, a well-written cover letter allows you to highlight key achievements, explain gaps in your resume, and express why you're passionate about the role and the company. It's your chance to make a memorable first impression, setting you apart from other applicants and persuading the hiring manager to give your application a closer look.

Remember, your cover letter is an opportunity to advocate for yourself. It's where you can argue convincingly why your skills, experiences, and values align with the company's needs and culture. By taking the time to craft a thoughtful and compelling cover letter, you significantly increase your chances of landing that coveted interview.

Personalizing Your Job Application: The Impact of a Cover Letter

Your cover letter is more than just a formal introduction—it's a personalized message to your potential employer. Unlike your resume, which lists your qualifications and work history in a structured format, your cover letter gives you the space to express your personality, enthusiasm, and specific interest in the company and the role you're applying for.

This personal touch is crucial in the job application process. It allows you to speak directly to the hiring manager, sharing your story and highlighting the unique qualities that make you the ideal candidate. By carefully crafting your cover letter, you can demonstrate not only your professional skills and achievements but also your ability to communicate effectively and your genuine passion for the job.

In your cover letter, you have the opportunity to explain why you're drawn to the company's mission or how your values align with its culture. You can share anecdotes or examples from your previous experiences that showcase your problem-solving skills, leadership qualities, or ability to work in a team—attributes that are often difficult to convey through a resume alone.

Moreover, a well-written cover letter can help you stand out in a crowded field of applicants. It's your chance to make a strong, positive impression before you've even met the hiring manager in person. By taking the time to personalize your cover letter, you're showing that you're not just interested in any job—you're specifically interested in this job, at this company. This level of detail and personalization can significantly enhance your job application, making it more likely that you'll be called in for an interview.

In essence, your cover letter is a powerful tool for

personalizing your job application. It's an invitation for potential employers to get to know you, not just as a list of qualifications, but as a motivated, passionate individual who's eager to contribute to their team.

PREPARATION BEFORE WRITING

Mastering the Homework: Researching Your Future Employer and Role

Before you even start typing out your cover letter, there's a crucial step you need to take: researching the company and the specific job role you're applying for. This isn't just about showing off how much you know in your letter; it's about understanding what the company really needs and how you can be the solution.

First, dive into the company's website. Look beyond the homepage. Explore their "About Us" section to grasp their mission, values, and history. What projects are they proud of? What language do they use to describe themselves? This insight will help you align your cover letter with their culture and values.

Next, check out their social media profiles and any recent news articles about them. These sources can provide a more dynamic picture of the company's current interests and challenges. Maybe they've just expanded into a new market, or they're focusing on sustainability. These details can provide great talking points in your letter.

For the specific job role, carefully read the job description. Identify the key skills and experiences they're looking for. But go further—try to read between the lines. What does the role entail on a day-to-day basis? What kind of person do they need? Understanding this can help you highlight the most relevant parts of your background.

Also, if possible, talk to someone who works at the company or in a similar role elsewhere. They can offer insights you won't find online—like what the team's really like or the challenges they're facing.

By doing your homework, you show potential employers that you're genuinely interested in the role and that you've taken the time to understand how you can contribute. Plus, it'll give you a solid foundation to tailor your cover letter (and later, your interview responses) to what the company truly needs. Remember, a well-researched application is often the one that stands out.

Crafting Your Key:
Matching Skills and
Experiences to the Job

When you're preparing to apply for a job, one of the most crucial steps is to identify and showcase the key skills and experiences that make you the perfect fit for the position. This doesn't just mean listing everything you've ever done. It's about selecting the gems that resonate most with the job you're eyeing.

Start with the job description. Employers often list the skills and experiences they're looking for in order of importance. Highlight these requirements and think about how your own background aligns with them. Have you led a team, managed a project, or exceeded sales goals? These are the kinds of experiences you want to highlight.

But don't stop at the obvious. Think about the soft skills that might not be directly mentioned but are critical for the role. For example, almost every job benefits from strong communication skills, problem-solving abilities, and adaptability. Reflect on times when you've demonstrated these skills and how they've contributed to your success in previous roles.

Consider your experiences outside of traditional employment, too. Volunteer work, side projects, and extracurricular activities can all provide valuable examples of your skills and dedication. Maybe you organized a fundraising event that required meticulous planning and teamwork, or perhaps you run a blog that showcases your writing skills and discipline.

It's also helpful to quantify your achievements when possible. Numbers can provide concrete evidence of your impact in previous roles. For example, "increased sales by 20%" or "reduced processing time by 30%" are strong indicators of your effectiveness.

Remember, the goal is to make it easy for the hiring manager to see you in the role. By carefully selecting and presenting your skills and experiences, you're not just listing your qualifications—you're telling a story about why you're the ideal candidate for the job. This approach can significantly boost your chances of landing an interview and ultimately, the job itself.

STRUCTURE OF A
COVER LETTER

*First Impressions Count:
Crafting a Strong Opening
for Your Cover Letter*

The opening of your cover letter is your first chance to grab the hiring manager's attention, making it one of the most critical parts of your application. A strong opening statement not only introduces you but also captivates the reader, compelling them to read on. Here's how you can start your cover letter on the right note.

Begin with a personal greeting whenever possible. Instead of a generic "To whom it may concern," try to find out the name of the hiring manager or the person responsible for reviewing applications. A simple "Dear [Name]" instantly makes your letter more personal and engaging.

Next, dive into why you're writing with enthusiasm and purpose. Start with a sentence that highlights your excitement about the opportunity. For example, "I was thrilled to come across the opening for [Job Title] at [Company Name], as I have long admired your commitment to [something you genuinely admire about the company]."

Follow this by briefly introducing yourself and stating the position you're applying for. Make sure to weave in a compelling reason why you are particularly interested in this role and this company. For instance, "With over [X years] of experience in [Your Field], I am eager to bring my expertise in [specific skills or areas] to your innovative team."

The key is to be concise but impactful. Your opening should not only inform the reader of your intentions but also hint at the value you can bring to the team. It's your first impression, so make it count by being genuine, enthusiastic, and focused on what you can offer.

Remember, the opening of your cover letter sets the tone for the rest of your message. By starting strong, you significantly increase your chances of keeping the hiring manager engaged and making them eager to learn more about you.

Building the Core: Structuring

the Body of Your Cover Letter

After captivating your reader with a strong opening, the body of your cover letter is where you delve into the heart of your application. This section is your opportunity to showcase why you're the perfect fit for the role by highlighting your relevant experiences, skills, and alignment with the company's goals and values. Here's how to structure this crucial part of your cover letter effectively.

1. Connect Your Experience to the Job Description: Start by selecting two to three key requirements from the job description that you fulfill exceptionally well. For each requirement, provide a specific example from your past experiences that demonstrates how you've successfully utilized the skill or achieved a relevant accomplishment. Use action verbs to start each example, and where possible, quantify your achievements to add credibility.

2. Demonstrate Your Soft Skills: In addition to your technical skills and experiences, highlight the soft skills that make you a well-rounded candidate for the role. Whether it's your ability to lead a team, your innovative problem-solving techniques, or your exceptional communication skills, choose examples that reflect how these attributes have positively impacted your previous workplaces.

3. Show Enthusiasm for the Role and Company: Employers want to hire candidates who are genuinely interested in their organization. Mention specific aspects of the company or role that excite you, and explain why. This could be the company's innovative approach to the industry, its commitment to sustainability, or the potential for personal growth the role offers. Demonstrating your enthusiasm and knowledge about the company will set you apart from candidates who are applying indiscriminately.

4. Explain Why You're a Great Fit: Wrap up the body of your cover letter by succinctly stating why your skills, experiences, and personal qualities make you an ideal fit for the job and the company culture. This is your chance to make a compelling argument for why the hiring manager should consider you for the position.

Formatting Tips:
Keep paragraphs short and easy to read.
Use bullet points for listing accomplishments or skills to improve readability.
Tailor each cover letter to the job and company, avoiding generic statements.

Remember, the body of your cover letter is your sales pitch. By carefully structuring it to highlight how your unique blend of skills and experiences aligns with the job you're applying for, you significantly increase your chances of making a memorable impression on the hiring manager.

The Perfect Sign-Off: Ending Your Cover Letter with Impact

Concluding your cover letter on a high note is crucial for leaving a lasting impression. The conclusion is your final opportunity to express your enthusiasm for the role and to encourage the hiring manager to take the next step. Here's how to craft a compelling ending to your cover letter that resonates with the reader.

Express Gratitude: Start your conclusion by thanking the hiring manager for considering your application. This not only shows your appreciation but also reinforces your interest in the position. A simple sentence like, "Thank you for taking the time to consider my application," sets a positive tone.

Reiterate Your Enthusiasm: Briefly restate why you are excited about the opportunity and why you believe you are the right fit for the role and the company. This reinforces your alignment with the company's goals and demonstrates your genuine interest. For instance, "I am truly excited about the opportunity to contribute my skills and expertise to [Company Name]'s innovative team, and I am confident in my ability to help achieve [specific company goal]."

Include a Call to Action: Rather than ending passively, encourage the hiring manager to take action. This could be inviting them to contact you for an interview, stating your intention to follow up, or expressing your willingness to provide further information. For example, "I look forward to the opportunity to discuss in more detail how I can contribute to the success of [Company Name]. Please feel free to contact me at [your phone number] or [your email] to schedule an interview."

Sign Off Professionally: Close your cover letter with a professional sign-off followed by your name. "Sincerely," "Best regards," or "Warmly" followed by your full name are all appropriate and convey respect and professionalism.

Example Conclusion:
"Thank you for considering my application. I am enthusiastic about the chance to bring my unique skills to [Company Name], contributing to your team's success and innovative projects. I look forward to the possibility of discussing this exciting opportunity with you. Please don't hesitate to contact me at [your contact information]. Sincerely, [Your Name]."

Remember, the conclusion of your cover letter is your last chance to make an impression, so make it count. By ending on a positive note and including a clear call to action, you increase the chances that the hiring manager will move forward with your application.

WRITING TIPS FOR A COMPELLING COVER LETTER

Making It Yours: The Art of Personalizing Your Cover Letter

Crafting a cover letter that stands out isn't just about showcasing your skills and experiences—it's about making a genuine connection with the job and the company you're applying to. Personalization is key in demonstrating that you're not just looking for any job, but specifically for this role at this company. Here's how you can tailor your cover letter to make a lasting impression.

Research the Company: Dive deep into the

company's website, social media channels, and recent news articles to understand its mission, culture, and recent achievements. This research will not only inform you about the company but also help you articulate why you're drawn to it.

Understand the Job Role: Analyze the job description carefully. Pay attention to the skills and experiences the company values most. Understanding the nuances of the role allows you to highlight the aspects of your background that are most relevant.

Reflect the Company's Language: Use the same language and tone found in the job listing and the company's communication materials. If the company uses a more casual tone, it's safe to slightly relax the formality of your language—without sacrificing professionalism.

Mention Specific Details: Show that you've done your homework by mentioning something specific about the company that excites you. It could be a project they're working on, a company value you share, or a recent achievement. Connecting your personal experiences or aspirations to these details demonstrates a deeper level of interest and engagement.

Explain Your Unique Fit: Use the body of your cover letter to explain why you, with your unique set of skills and experiences, are the perfect fit for the job.

Go beyond what's on your resume to tell a story that illustrates your suitability for the role.

Example:
"After researching [Company Name] and learning about your commitment to [specific company value or project], I was inspired to apply. My experience with [specific skill or project related to what you learned about the company] aligns with your team's goals, and I am excited about the opportunity to contribute to your success."

Customize Every Time: While it might be tempting to use a template, remember that every job and company is different. Taking the time to customize your cover letter for each application shows that you're genuinely interested and willing to put in the effort.

In conclusion, personalization is the key to a cover letter that resonates with hiring managers. By tailoring your letter to the job and company, you demonstrate your enthusiasm, commitment, and the unique value you bring to the role. This approach not only sets you apart from other candidates but also lays the groundwork for a meaningful conversation during your interview.

Clear and Concise: The Key

to Effective Cover Letters

When crafting your cover letter, clarity and conciseness are your best allies. This approach ensures that your message is not only understood but also appreciated by busy hiring managers who sift through numerous applications. Here's how you can keep your cover letter focused and to the point, ensuring it makes the impact you desire.

Start with Structure: Before you begin writing, outline the main points you want to cover. This might include a brief introduction, a summary of your most relevant experiences, a discussion of your skills, and a conclusion with a call to action. Having a clear structure in mind helps you stay on topic and avoid veering off into less relevant details.

Be Specific: Instead of making broad statements about your abilities or experiences, zero in on specific examples that demonstrate your qualifications for the job. This not only adds credibility to your claims but also keeps your content focused and impactful.

Use Active Language: Active voice makes your writing more direct and dynamic. Phrases like "I led a team" or "I increased sales" are clear and concise, directly showcasing your contributions and achievements.

Eliminate Redundancies: Watch out for phrases or sentences that don't add new information. If you find yourself repeating points or using multiple examples for the same skill, choose the strongest one and cut the rest. This will help keep your letter concise and engaging.

Limit Your Length: Aim for no more than one page. This constraint forces you to distill your message to its essence, focusing on the most compelling content. If you're struggling to fit everything into this space, take another look at what you've included. Every sentence should serve a purpose in illustrating why you're the right candidate for the job.

Edit Ruthlessly: Once you've drafted your cover letter, take the time to edit it with a critical eye. Look for opportunities to streamline your writing and clarify your points. Removing unnecessary words and phrases can dramatically improve the readability and effectiveness of your letter.

Example:
"Thank you for considering my application for the [Job Title] position at [Company Name]. With [X years] of experience in [Field], particularly in [specific task or project], I am excited about the opportunity to contribute to your team's success."

Remember, your cover letter is a professional document intended to introduce you and highlight your suitability for the role. By keeping it clear and concise, you respect the reader's time while effectively communicating your enthusiasm and qualifications. This approach not only demonstrates your ability to convey information efficiently but also leaves a lasting, positive impression.

Striking the Balance: Professional Yet Engaging Cover Letters

Crafting a cover letter that is both professional and engaging is key to capturing the attention of hiring managers. Your cover letter is not just a formality; it's an opportunity to make a compelling case for your candidacy. Achieving the right tone can set you apart from the competition and make a memorable impression. Here's how you can maintain a professional tone while still engaging your reader.

Focus on Your Word Choice: Opt for language that is formal enough to convey professionalism but accessible enough to keep the reader engaged. Avoid slang and overly casual expressions, but don't be afraid to show some personality, especially if it aligns with the company's culture.

Be Enthusiastic but Sincere: Express genuine enthusiasm for the role and the company. Let your excitement shine through by mentioning specific aspects of the job or organization that particularly appeal to you. However, ensure your enthusiasm comes across as sincere rather than exaggerated.

Use Active Voice: Writing in an active voice contributes to a more dynamic and direct cover letter. Sentences like "I led a team" or "I achieved a 20% increase in sales" are clear and assertive, showcasing your achievements without over embellishment.

Be Respectful and Courteous: Always address the hiring manager or the recipient of your letter respectfully. If you know their name, use it. If not, opt for a general yet respectful salutation like "Dear Hiring Manager." Remember to thank the reader for their time and consideration at the end of your letter.

Showcase Your Professionalism Through Examples: Instead of merely stating that you're a professional, demonstrate it through specific examples of your work experience and achievements. This approach lends credibility to your claims and illustrates your professional demeanor.

Edit for Tone and Clarity: Reread your cover letter

to ensure it strikes the right balance between professionalism and engagement. Ask yourself if it sounds like something you would confidently present in a professional setting while still keeping the reader interested.

Example:
"Dear [Hiring Manager's Name],
I am writing to express my interest in the [Job Title] position at [Company Name]. With a solid background in [Your Field], including notable achievements such as [specific achievement], I am excited about the opportunity to bring my expertise to your team. [Company Name]'s commitment to [something you admire about the company] resonates deeply with my professional values and aspirations.Thank you for considering my application. I look forward to the possibility of discussing how I can contribute to the continued success and growth of [Company Name].
Sincerely,
[Your Name]"

By maintaining a professional yet engaging tone, your cover letter will not only demonstrate your suitability for the role but also showcase your ability to communicate effectively. This balance is crucial for making a positive first impression and advancing to the next stage of the hiring process.

The Final Polish: Why Proofreading Your Cover Letter is Essential

Before you hit send on your job application, there's one crucial step left: proofreading your cover letter. Even the most compelling cover letter can be undermined by a simple spelling mistake or grammar error. Taking the time to review your letter not only ensures it's polished and professional but also shows your attention to detail —a trait highly valued by employers. Here's why proofreading is an indispensable part of crafting your cover letter.

Catch Common Mistakes: Even the best writers can make simple errors, especially when they've been working closely with a document. A thorough proofread allows you to catch and correct common mistakes in spelling, grammar, and punctuation that could otherwise distract from your message.

Ensure Clarity and Flow: Proofreading isn't just about spotting errors; it's also an opportunity to ensure your cover letter is clear, concise, and logically structured. Read your letter out loud to catch awkward phrasing or sentences that don't flow well. This step helps ensure your key points are communicated effectively.

Verify Accuracy: Double-check the accuracy of key details such as the company name, the hiring manager's name, and the position you're applying for. Mistakes in these areas can indicate a lack of attention to detail and could potentially disqualify you from consideration.

Maintain Professionalism: A well-proofread cover letter reflects your professionalism and dedication. It shows the hiring manager that you take the opportunity seriously and are committed to making the best possible impression.

Tips for Effective Proofreading:

Take a break before proofreading: Stepping away from your cover letter for a little while can give you a fresh perspective when you return to it.

Read out loud: This can help you catch errors that you might miss when reading silently.

Use spellcheck, but don't rely on it entirely: Automated tools can miss context-specific errors or autocorrect mistakes.

Ask a friend or mentor to review it: A second pair of eyes can catch errors you've overlooked and provide valuable feedback.

Proofreading your cover letter is the final step in ensuring that your application is as strong as it can be. By dedicating time to this process, you're not only avoiding potential pitfalls but also reinforcing your commitment to excellence. Remember, your cover letter is often your first introduction to a potential employer—make sure it's a flawless one.

COMMON MISTAKES TO AVOID

Custom Fit: The Pitfall of Generic Cover Letters

In the world of job applications, sending a generic, one-size-fits-all cover letter is like wearing a suit that hasn't been tailored—it simply won't make the best impression. Customizing your cover letter for each job application is crucial in demonstrating your genuine interest in the position and the company. Here's why avoiding generic cover letters is important and how tailoring each one can significantly boost your chances of getting noticed.

Show You Care: A generic cover letter can make it seem like you're sending out applications without much thought or effort. On the other hand, a personalized cover letter shows that you've taken the time to research the company and understand the role. It tells the hiring manager that you're truly interested in this specific opportunity, not just any job.

Stand Out from the Crowd: Hiring managers can spot a generic cover letter from a mile away. When you tailor your letter, you distinguish yourself from other applicants who may not have put in the same level of effort. This can be particularly effective in competitive job markets, where standing out from the crowd is essential.

Highlight Relevant Skills and Experiences: Each job has unique requirements, and a one-size-fits-all cover letter won't adequately showcase how your specific skills and experiences make you the best fit for the role. By customizing your cover letter, you can highlight the most relevant aspects of your background, demonstrating clearly why you're a strong candidate for this particular position.

Demonstrate Your Knowledge of the Company: A personalized cover letter allows you to express your enthusiasm for the company and its mission, culture, or projects. Mentioning specific details about the company shows that you've done your homework and are genuinely interested in becoming part of their team.

Avoiding the Generic Trap:

Always start with the hiring manager's name if you can find it.

Mention the specific job title and how you learned about the opening.

Include a sentence or two about why the company attracts you.

Tailor the skills and experiences you highlight to match the job description.

Example:

"Dear [Hiring Manager's Name],

I was excited to see the opening for [Job Title] at [Company Name] listed on [where you found the job listing]. Your commitment to [specific company value or project] resonates deeply with my professional values and experience, particularly my background in [specific relevant experience]."

By taking the time to craft a customized cover letter for each application, you not only increase your chances of catching the hiring manager's eye but also demonstrate your commitment and enthusiasm for the role. Remember, a little effort goes a long way in making a lasting impression.

Keeping It Professional: What Not to Include in

Your Cover Letter

When crafting your cover letter, it's essential to strike the right balance between being informative and oversharing. While you want to provide a comprehensive view of your qualifications and enthusiasm for the role, there are certain details that are best left out. Here's a guide on what information to omit from your cover letter to keep it professional and focused.

Personal Life Details: While it's tempting to share personal stories or challenges to illustrate your qualities or resilience, your cover letter should primarily focus on your professional experiences and skills. Unless a personal aspect directly impacts your professional life or is specifically relevant to the job, it's better to leave it out.

Negative Experiences with Previous Employers: Speaking negatively about your past employers or colleagues can come off as unprofessional. Instead, focus on what you've learned from your experiences and how they've prepared you for the role you're applying for.

Salary Expectations: Unless the job posting explicitly asks for your salary requirements, it's advisable to leave this topic for later in the hiring process. Prematurely discussing salary can give the impression that compensation is your only interest.

Generic Statements: Phrases like "I'm a hard worker" or "I'm a fast learner" without specific examples or evidence can sound insincere and take up valuable space. Focus on highlighting concrete achievements and skills that demonstrate your capabilities.

Irrelevant Achievements: While it's important to showcase your accomplishments, ensure they are relevant to the job you're applying for. Achievements that don't relate to the role might distract from your pertinent qualifications.

Too Much Humility: While modesty is a virtue, downplaying your achievements or skills too much can make you seem underqualified. Be confident in presenting your qualifications and how they align with the job requirements.

Example:
"Instead of focusing on personal hobbies or unrelated achievements, I have concentrated my cover letter on demonstrating my proven track record in [specific professional skill or achievement] and my keen interest in contributing to [Company Name]'s success, particularly in your efforts to [specific company project or goal]."

Remember, your cover letter is a professional document aimed at showcasing your qualifications and fit for the role. By carefully selecting what to include and what to leave out, you ensure that your cover letter is compelling, focused, and leaves a positive impression on the hiring manager.

Stay Positive: The Power of Optimistic Language in Your Cover Letter

In the journey of job applications, your cover letter is your moment to shine. It's where you make your first impression, and as the saying goes, you never get a second chance to make a first impression. This is why maintaining a positive and confident tone in your cover letter is crucial. Here's how to ensure your language uplifts and propels you forward in the eyes of the hiring manager.

Focus on What You Can Do: Instead of highlighting what you haven't done or skills you lack, concentrate on showcasing your abilities and achievements. Use your cover letter to talk about your successes, the challenges you've overcome, and the unique skills you bring to the table.

Turn Negatives into Positives: If you feel compelled to address a gap in your employment or a shift in your career path, frame it in a positive light. Discuss what you learned during that time or how it has prepared you for the next step in your career. For example, "The time I spent away from the workforce allowed me to develop a fresh perspective and acquire new skills that I'm eager to apply in this role."

Use Positive Language: Words have power. Choose language that reflects optimism, enthusiasm, and confidence. Phrases like "I'm excited by the opportunity to..." or "I'm passionate about..." convey your eagerness and positive outlook. Avoid phrases that diminish your experiences or qualifications, such as "I just..." or "I only..."

Be Solution-Oriented: When discussing past challenges or projects, focus on the solutions you found and the results you achieved. This approach not only demonstrates your problem-solving skills but also your ability to remain positive and proactive in the face of obstacles.

Express Gratitude: A simple thank you can go a long way. Expressing gratitude for the reader's time and consideration shows your appreciation and leaves a positive impression.

Example:
"I am truly excited about the opportunity to bring my unique blend of skills and experiences to the [Job Title] position at [Company Name]. I am particularly

drawn to this role because of [Company Name]'s commitment to [something you admire about the company], and I am eager to contribute to your team's success."

By keeping the tone of your cover letter positive and confident, you not only demonstrate your professional demeanor but also your resilience and enthusiasm for the role. This optimistic approach can make your application memorable and increase your chances of landing an interview.

ADVANCED TIPS

Template to Triumph:
Crafting Your Perfect
Cover Letter

In the process of job hunting, creating a standout cover letter for each application can seem daunting. However, using a template as a foundation can simplify this task and help you craft a compelling cover letter that captures attention. Here's how a template can be your ally in presenting yourself as the ideal candidate for the job.

Structured Framework: A template provides a clear structure for your cover letter, ensuring that you include all the essential elements, such as the introduction, body, and conclusion. This organization helps you present your information logically, making it easier for hiring managers to follow.

Saves Time: With a template, you don't have to start from scratch for each application. It serves as a customizable blueprint that you can adapt to different roles and companies. This efficiency allows you to focus more on tailoring the content to fit the specific job you're applying for.

Consistency and Professionalism: A well-designed template ensures that your cover letter maintains a professional appearance, with consistent formatting, font, and spacing. This visual consistency is important as it reflects your attention to detail and professionalism.

Focus on Content: With the basic format taken care of, you can concentrate on refining the content of your cover letter. This means you can spend more time personalizing your letter, highlighting your skills, experiences, and why you're a great fit for the role and the company.

Avoids Common Mistakes: Templates can also help steer you away from common pitfalls, such as overly long paragraphs or forgetting to include a call to action. By following a template, you're reminded of best practices in cover letter writing.

Encourages Personalization: While a template provides the basic outline, it's essential to customize your cover letter for each job application. Use the template as a guide, but make sure to inject your personality and specific details about your experiences and achievements that align with the job you're applying for.

In summary, a cover letter template is a powerful tool in your job application arsenal. It streamlines the writing process, ensuring your cover letters are structured, professional, and tailored to each application. By leveraging a template, you can effectively showcase your qualifications and enthusiasm for the role, making a strong case for why you should be the next great addition to the team.

Keyword Connection: Tailoring Your Cover Letter with Precision

In today's competitive job market, tailoring your cover letter by incorporating keywords from the job description can significantly enhance your application's visibility and relevance. This strategic approach ensures your cover letter speaks directly to what the hiring manager is looking for. Here's how and why using keywords from the job description can set you apart.

Why Keywords Matter: Many companies use

Applicant Tracking Systems (ATS) to sift through the high volume of applications they receive. These systems scan cover letters and resumes for specific keywords related to the job posting. By including these keywords in your cover letter, you increase your chances of getting past the ATS and catching the hiring manager's eye.

How to Identify Keywords: Carefully read the job description and note the skills, qualifications, and attributes mentioned. Look for repeated phrases or unique terms that describe the role's responsibilities or the company's culture. These are your keywords. They can range from technical skills and job titles to soft skills and industry-specific terms.

Incorporating Keywords Naturally: Once you've identified the keywords, the next step is to weave them into your cover letter naturally. This doesn't mean stuffing your letter with as many keywords as possible; instead, integrate them thoughtfully into the narrative of your professional experiences and achievements. Show how your background aligns with the job requirements by using the same language the company uses.

Example:
"If the job description emphasizes a need for 'strong project management skills' and experience with 'cross-functional teams,' you might write: 'In my previous role, I honed my project management skills

by leading cross-functional teams to successfully deliver complex projects on tight deadlines.'"

Beyond the ATS: While getting past the ATS is important, remember that your cover letter's ultimate goal is to resonate with the human reader. Use keywords to create a compelling narrative that demonstrates you're not just a match on paper but also genuinely enthusiastic and prepared to contribute to the company's success.

Demonstrate Understanding and Fit: By using keywords, you're also showing that you've taken the time to understand the company and the role. This level of personalization and attention to detail can make a strong impression on hiring managers, suggesting that you're a thoughtful and dedicated candidate.

In essence, incorporating keywords from the job description into your cover letter is a powerful way to align your application with the specific needs and language of the company. This tailored approach not only helps your cover letter stand out but also demonstrates your keen interest in the role and your fit for the position.

Bridging the Gaps:

Addressing Concerns in
Your Cover Letter

At times, your resume might not tell the full story of your professional journey. Gaps in employment, a shift in career paths, or a lack of specific experience might raise questions for potential employers. However, your cover letter offers a perfect opportunity to address these concerns head-on, turning potential weaknesses into demonstrations of strength, resilience, and adaptability. Here's how you can effectively address any gaps or concerns in your cover letter.

Acknowledge Gaps Honestly: If there's a noticeable gap in your employment history, briefly acknowledge it and focus on how that time was spent positively. Whether it was due to personal reasons, further education, or exploring a new career direction, explain how this period contributed to your personal and professional growth.

Example: "During the year-long break between my previous positions, I dedicated myself to professional development, taking online courses in [specific skills] and volunteering at [organization], where I gained valuable experience in [relevant experience]."

Highlight Transferable Skills: Career changes or

diverse job experiences can be seen as assets rather than liabilities. Focus on the transferable skills you've acquired from different roles and how they make you uniquely qualified for the position you're applying for.

Example: "Transitioning from a career in [Previous Career] to [Target Career], I have honed skills such as [transferable skill 1], [transferable skill 2], and [transferable skill 3], which are directly applicable to the [Job Title] role at your company."

Emphasize Continuous Learning: Employers value candidates who are committed to learning and self-improvement. If you're lacking in direct experience, discuss how you've taken steps to bridge that gap through additional training, courses, or self-study.

Example: "Aware of my limited experience in [specific area], I proactively enrolled in [course or training] to enhance my understanding and capabilities, preparing me to contribute effectively to your team."

Showcase Resilience and Adaptability: Use your cover letter to demonstrate how facing challenges head-on has made you a more resilient and adaptable professional. This can turn a potential concern into a testament to your character and work ethic.

Example: "Faced with [specific challenge], I adapted by [action taken], resulting in [positive outcome], which further developed my resilience and ability to thrive in changing environments."

Connect the Dots: Make it easy for hiring managers to see how your unique experiences have equipped you with a diverse skill set that can bring fresh perspectives and innovative solutions to their team.

Example: "My varied background in [previous roles] has not only enriched my skill set but has also given me a unique perspective that I am excited to bring to the [specific role] at [Company Name]."

Addressing potential concerns or gaps in your resume through your cover letter allows you to control the narrative. By focusing on your strengths, adaptability, and the positive aspects of your professional journey, you can turn potential weaknesses into compelling reasons to hire you.

WRAPPING IT UP: THE KEY TO UNLOCKING YOUR NEXT OPPORTUNITY

We've journeyed through the essentials of crafting a compelling cover letter, from understanding its purpose and structure to personalizing it for each job application. We've discussed the importance of starting with a strong opening, showcasing your skills and experiences in the body, and wrapping up with a confident conclusion. Along the way, we've emphasized the value of tailoring your message, using keywords from the job description, and demonstrating your knowledge of the company's values and mission.

Crafting a personalized cover letter for each

application may seem like a significant investment of time, but it's an investment in your future. A well-crafted cover letter can set you apart from the competition, showcasing not just your qualifications but your passion and unique personality. It's your first opportunity to make a strong impression on a potential employer, an invitation for them to get to know you better and see the value you would bring to their team.

Remember, your cover letter is more than just a formality; it's a powerful tool in your job search arsenal. By investing the time to customize and polish your cover letter for each application, you're not only increasing your chances of landing an interview but also demonstrating your commitment and attention to detail. This effort can make all the difference in making a strong first impression that leads to your next great job opportunity.

So, take these tips, apply them with care, and approach each cover letter as a chance to shine. Your future starts with this one small step, and who knows where it might lead? With a bit of effort and a lot of heart, your perfect cover letter could be the key that unlocks the door to your next big adventure.